PEARLS *of*
Wisdom

TOYOSHA UPSHAW

Introduction

This is the second book of Wisdom for Worldly Living. This book, Pearls of Wisdom, is also dedicated to my nieces and nephews. Some lessons are learned from trials and tribulations whereas others from shared wisdom. I am choosing to share the wisdom I've gained from blood, sweat and tears so you don't have to travel down those tough paths. History does repeat itself so be prepared.

My prayer is that this book bless you for years and generations to come.

Continuous love, prayer and blessings to all.

Contents

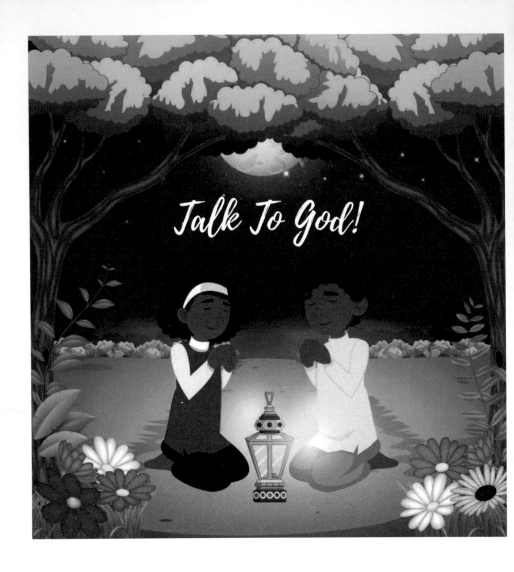

The Lord is near to all who call on him, to all who call on him in truth. Psalm 145:18

You have to learn the voice of God so you don't fall victim to the devil's tricks.

Developing a personal relationship with God will be the most important relationship ever. Allow God to recognize your voice.

Talk to God daily and continuously and leave time open to hear his plans and desires for you. Tell him your thoughts and receive comfort in his word.

Seek the Lord while He may be found;
call on him while He is near. Isaiah 55:6

Life Is About Choices!

Rejoicing in Hope; patient in tribulation; continuing instant in prayer. Romans 12:12

Life may not always go according to *your* plan.

Look for the good in delays and detours; stumbling blocks and road blocks serve a purpose. Sometimes they are used to slow us down or to keep us from a path of destruction.

Many are the plans in the mind of man, but it is the purpose of the Lord that will stand. Proverbs 19:21

And we know that in all things God works for the good of those who love him, who have been called according to his purpose. Romans 8:28

Always have a plan.

If you don't have a plan then you plan to fail. Have a backup plan in case things go awry.

While planning, exhaust all solutions and possibilities to help make the best decision.

Change the plan but not your goal!

Suppose one of you wants to build a tower. Won't you first sit down and estimate the cost to see if you have enough money to complete it? Luke 14:28

Brethren, I count not myself to have apprehended: but {this} one thing {I do}, forgetting those things which are behind, and reaching forth unto those things which are before. Philippians 3:13

I made mistakes but I learned from every one. Tupac Shakur

Everyone can attest to making a bad choice. Even though bad decisions cost us time, money and sanity; we must Learn.

Lessons can be expensive but worthwhile to avoid making the same mistake again.

If you had not learned a lesson then you will not have gained the knowledge.

For the righteous falls seven times and rises again, but the wicked stumble in times of calamity. Proverbs24:16

Choose Wisely, Friends
And Enemies!

Do not be misled: Bad company corrupts good character. 1 Corinthians 15:33

If a friend turns enemy then they were never your friend. Tupac Shakur

Show me your friends and I will show you your future. In life you will have many associates and few true friends.

Everybody is not your friend. Don't allow someone to hang around longer than necessary or you will prolong receiving your blessing.

Enter through the narrow gate. For wide is the gate and broad is the road that leads to destruction, and many enter through it. Matthew 7:13

And that ye study to be quiet, and to do your own business, and to work with your own hands, as we have commanded you. 1 Thessalonians 4:11

To thine own self be true.

There is a difference in secretive and private, secretive is sneaky and hiding things, privacy is setting boundaries.

Don't share major things with minor people. Your business should not be show business.

If you don't want anyone to know then tell no one, protect your sanity.

Besides that, they learn to be idlers,
going about from house to house,
and not only idlers, but also gossips
and busybodies, saying what they
should not. 1 Timothy 5:13

Gossips!

A hypocrite with his mouth destroyeth
his neighbor: but through knowledge
shall the just be delivered. Proverbs 11:9

Don't be fooled. Guys gossip just as much as girls!

Some people are double agents, they hang with you only to find out your business to repeat it. If someone tells you another person business then they are telling another your business.

Some people will be gossips, users, jealous-hearted or just offer bad advice but God will never lead you down the wrong path.

A gossip betrays a confidence:
so avoid anyone who talks too
much. Proverbs 20:19

For the love of money is the root of all kinds of evil. Some people, eager for money, have wandered from the faith and pierced themselves with many griefs. Timothy 6:10

If you have fifty two rooms then you should give one room to someone who has none. Tupac Shakur

The Bible states that if you have not charity then you have nothing.

The most important things in life, money can't buy: peace, joy, love and life.

The Bible states it is hard for a rich man to make it into heaven; it's not impossible just hard because most trust in their riches and not God.

Then he said to them, "Watch out!
Be on your guard against all kinds
of greed; life does not consist in
abundance of possessions." Luke 12:15

To every thing there is a season,
and a time to every purpose under
the heaven. *Ecclesiastes 3:1*

Everything and everyone serves a purpose in your life.

Even the best relationships end.

Learn the lesson, gain the patience, and find peace and joy.

Embrace the time and move forward, be a better person because of the event, situation or person.

Preach the word, be ready in season and out of season; reprove, rebuke, and exhort, with complete patience and teaching. 2 Timothy 4:2

But the Comforter, which is the Holy Ghost, whom the Father will send in my name, he shall teach you all things, and bring all things to your remembrance, whatsoever I have said unto you. John 14:26

You can never make a bad choice listening to the Holy Spirit.

Trust your gut instinct; it is a gift from God.

The Holy Spirit will challenge, convict, and comfort you so that you will become Christ-like.

And I will ask the Father, and he will
give you another advocate to help you
and be with you forever. John 14:16

11451276R00018